P9-DXM-123

Birdhousing

Birdhousing

PERI
WOLFMAN

CHARLES
GOLD

Clarkson Potter/Publishers
New York

Published by Clarkson N. Potter, Inc., 201 East 50th Street,
New York, New York 10022. Member of the Crown Publishing Group.
Random House, Inc. New York, Toronto, London, Sydney, Auckland
Clarkson N. Potter, Potter, and colophon are trademarks of
Clarkson N. Potter, Inc.
Manufactured in China
Design by Rita Marshall

Library of Congress Cataloging-in-Publication Data
Wolfman, Peri. Birdhousing / Peri Wolfman and Charles Gold.
Includes bibliographical references.
1. Birdhouses—Design and construction.   2. Bird feeders—Design
and construction.   3. Birds, Attracting of.   4. Birdhouses—
Collectors and collecting.   5. Bird feeders—Collectors and
collecting.   I. Gold, Charles.   II. Title.
QL676.5.W58   1993   598'.07234—DC20   92-1607

ISBN 0-517-58827-7

1   3   5   7   9   10   8   6   4   2

First Edition

To our four sons, Erik,

Benjy, Alexander, and

Jeremy, who we hope

someday will have

houses as cozy as the

ones in this book.

ACKNOWLEDGMENTS

WE HAVE FOUND WHILE RESEARCHING THIS BOOK THAT THERE IS VERY LITTLE WRITTEN INFORMATION ON BIRDHOUSES. IT'S A BIT HERE, A SENTENCE THERE, AND A LOT OF LORE FROM THE FOLKS WHO ARE BUILDING, COLLECTING, AND EXHIBITING BIRDHOUSES TODAY. WE COULD NOT HAVE PUT WORDS TO OUR PHOTOS WITHOUT THEIR ENTHUSIASM AND KNOWLEDGE, WHICH THEY GENEROUSLY SHARED WITH US.

OUR THANKS TO THE BUILDERS WHO LAID THE FOUNDATION FOR THIS BOOK: LAURA FOREMAN, PEGGY FRUEHLING & BILL GOODRICH, DEAN JOHNSON & JIMMY CRAMER, FERN LETNES, IRENE & PETER RUGGIERA, AND DEBBY & FRED VAN ANDA.

TO THE COLLECTORS WHO SET THE CORNERSTONES: AARNE ANTON, JOHN BARHAM & RICHARD AUER, ROBERT CURREY, MARTIN JACOBS, NEIL MUSSALLEM, AND LYN PETERSON.

TO OUR FRIENDS AND COLLEAGUES WHO PROVIDED THE DOORS AND WINDOWS: LEE BAILEY, JUDY COOK, MARY EMMERLING, BETTY ENG, LEO & BERTHA LA FONTANA, ELSIE LEVINE, SHARRON LEWIS, JOHN MACCHIO, SUSAN MEISEL, KATHY MOA, AND KAY TOWNE.

AND A VERY SPECIAL THANKS TO THE ARCHITECTS WHO GAVE *BIRD-HOUSING* ITS FORM AND SHAPE: PAM BERNSTEIN, ROY FINAMORE, RITA MARSHALL, AND SUSAN SPENCE.

CONTENTS

PREFACE

MANY YEARS AGO, IN THE EARLY SPRING — THAT TIME

OF YEAR NEW ENGLANDERS CALL MUD SEASON, WHEN

YOU CAN'T WAIT FOR THE GRASS TO TURN GREEN —

CHARLEY AND I BOUGHT A BIRDHOUSE. WE WERE

DRIVING BACK FROM COUNTRY TO CITY, FROM WEEK-

END PLAY TO MONDAY MORNING AT WORK, WHEN WE

SAW A SMALL FIELD FILLED WITH BRIGHT WHITE BIRD-

HOUSES. THERE WAS NO SIGN, NO INDICATION THAT

THESE DOZEN OR SO BIRDHOUSES, PERCHED ON POSTS

AND ON BENCHES, MIGHT BE FOR SALE, BUT WE DROVE

UP TO THE SMALL HOUSE ANYWAY. OUT CAME PETE, WEARING AN ARMY CAP AND CAMOUFLAGE JACKET, TO WELCOME US. HE WAS HAPPY THAT WE WANTED TO BUY ONE OF HIS TWO-STORY BIRDHOUSES. THEY WERE FOR MARTINS, PETE TOLD US, A BIRD THAT LIKES TO LIVE CLOSELY WITH OTHERS OF ITS SPECIES IN MULTI-STORY APARTMENT HOUSES. THAT WAS OUR FIRST BIRDHOUSE.

WE DIDN'T BUY JUST ONE; WE FILLED OUR VAN WITH THEM. ONE FOR US, ONE A BIRTHDAY GIFT FOR OUR FRIEND JOE, AND THE REST WENT TO OUR STORE FOR DISPLAY—AND LATER FOR SALE. THAT WAS THE START OF OUR INTEREST IN BIRDHOUSING. SINCE THEN WE'VE FOUND DOZENS OF HOUSES TO KEEP IN OUR CITY APARTMENT AND COUNTRY FARMHOUSE AND TO SELL IN OUR STORE.

BIRDHOUSES—OLD AND NEW, CRAFT AND ARCHITECTURAL—BECAME ONE OF OUR FAVORITE THINGS TO SEARCH FOR. PEOPLE STARTED COMING TO US OUT OF THE WOODS AND FIELDS. A FRIEND CON-

SULTED US ON THE DEVELOPMENT OF A GROUP OF

ARCHITECTURAL BIRDHOUSES THAT SHE WAS DESIGN-

ING FOR THE MINNESOTA DEPARTMENT OF ECONOMIC

DEVELOPMENT. THE QUESTION SHE ASKED WAS, "WHAT

COLOR SHOULD THEY BE PAINTED? SHOULD THEY BE

DECORATED?" OUR ANSWER WAS, "KEEP THEM SIMPLE;

PAINT THEM WHITE." AND SO THEY WERE, AND THEY

HAVE BECOME ONE OF THE MOST ELEGANT AND TIME-

LESS BIRDHOUSE COLLECTIONS OF THE LAST DECADE.

ALTHOUGH WE HAVE BROUGHT SOME OF OUR PRET-

TIEST AND MOST CHERISHED ANTIQUE BIRDHOUSES

INSIDE BECAUSE THEY ARE TOO OLD TO SURVIVE OUT-

SIDE ANY LONGER, THEY ARE REALLY ALL FOR THE

BIRDS. WE HAVE LEFT PIECES OF STRAW AND FEATHERS

POKING OUT OF THE ENTRY HOLES, PROVING TO OUR-

SELVES THAT THIS WAS INDEED BIRDHOUSING.

WE'RE NOT ALONE IN BRINGING BIRDHOUSING

INDOORS. YOU CAN HARDLY OPEN A DECORATING

MAGAZINE WITHOUT SEEING A COLLECTION OF BIRD-

HOUSES TUCKED INTO A BOOKSHELF OF A CITY APART-
MENT, OR A BIRD MANSION ON THE COFFEE TABLE OF A
COUNTRY HOUSE. OUTSIDE, TOO, BIRDHOUSING
BRINGS AN ARCHITECTURAL ELEMENT TO THE GARDEN,
A SURPRISE, LIKE A GARDEN BENCH WELL PLACED AND
HIDDEN AMONG THE FOLIAGE. THERE IS A ROMANTIC
SATISFACTION IN PROTECTING AND SAVING THESE
HOMEY RELICS OF A SIMPLER TIME LONG AGO.

WHAT ATTRACTS A BIRD TO NEST IN A HOUSE? THE
SHAPE AND SIZE OF THE OPENING HOLE, THE PLACE-
MENT OF THE HOUSE IN THE GARDEN, EVEN THE
COLOR OF THE HOUSE—THIS IS WHAT DETERMINES
WHAT SPECIES OF NESTING BIRD WILL MAKE A PARTICU-
LAR HOUSE ITS HOME.

IN THE COUNTRY WE PUT SMALL, SIMPLE BIRD-
HOUSES ON EACH POST OF OUR PICKET FENCE. THE
POSTS ARE ONLY FOUR FEET HIGH, WHICH IS MUCH
TOO LOW FOR THE LIKES OF MOST BIRDS, AND OUR

LITTLE PICKET-FENCED YARD IS VERY BUSY WITH GATES

OPENING AND CLOSING AS WE GO FROM THE GARDEN

TO THE KITCHEN. THESE BIRDHOUSES WERE GOING TO

BE STRICTLY DECORATIVE—SO WE THOUGHT. IMAG-

INE OUR SURPRISE ONE SPRING MORNING WHEN WE

TURNED ON THE SPRINKLER AND A TREE SWALLOW

FLEW OUT OF ONE HOUSE. OFF WENT THE SPRINKLER,

AND HAPPILY A FAMILY OF BABY SWALLOWS STAYED DRY

AND GREW UP TO FLY AWAY IN THE SUMMER. BUT NOT

WITHOUT OUR ENJOYING THEM AND CHARLEY PHOTO-

GRAPHING THEM THAT SPRING AND SUMMER.

WE ALSO HAVE LOTS OF BIRDHOUSES PERCHED ON

HIGH POSTS AT THE EDGE OF FIELDS—JUST THE WAY

THE BIRDS LIKE THEM. BUT SOME BIRDS DON'T GO FOR

CONVENTIONAL HOUSES. LAST SPRING A FAMILY OF

BARN SWALLOWS, TRUE TO THEIR NAME, BUILT THEIR

NEST ON TOP OF OUR BARN DOOR, JUST UNDER THE

EAVES — A NICE, COZY DRY PLACE FOR BABIES TO HATCH AND GROW UP. OF COURSE, WE COULDN'T OPEN THE BARN DOOR UNTIL THE BABIES WERE BIG ENOUGH TO FLY, BUT THIS WAS A SMALL INCONVENIENCE COMPARED TO THE PLEASURE WE HAD IN WATCHING THE PARENTS BUILD THEIR NEST AND BUSILY BRING FOOD TO THE BABIES, AND FINALLY SEEING THE YOUNG BIRDS FLY OFF ON THEIR OWN.

EXPERIENCES LIKE THESE HAVE ONLY MADE OUR INTEREST IN BIRDHOUSING MORE KEEN. WE ARE EXCITED WHEN WE SEE A NEW AND UNIQUE HOUSE, ANTIQUE OR NEWLY BUILT, FOR INSIDE OR OUT. WE ARE POSITIVELY THRILLED WHEN WE FIND THAT A BIRD HAS MADE A HOME IN ANY ONE OF OUR HOUSES IN THE GARDEN. AND WE LOVE OWNING LOTS OF HOUSES IN EVERY ARCHITECTURAL STYLE WE EVER DREAMED OF.

PERI WOLFMAN
BERKSHIRE COUNTY
MASSACHUSETTS

THE
BASIC
BIRDHOUSE

LIKE THE ONE-ROOM SCHOOLHOUSE, THE BASIC

BIRDHOUSE IS A PLAIN BOXLIKE STRUCTURE WITH A

PITCHED ROOF, A FRONT DOOR, AND LITTLE ELSE

TO ADORN IT. IT'S THE GENERIC HOUSE LITTLE

CHILDREN FIRST LEARN TO DRAW.

AND IT IS WITH THIS BASIC HOUSE

THAT BIRDHOUSE BUILDING

BEGINS.

EARLY
FARMER-BUILT
HOUSES

THE AMERICAN TRADITION OF BUILDING RUSTIC BIRD-

HOUSES WAS BORN OUT OF NECESSITY LONG AGO

WHEN EARLY SETTLERS STARTED FARMING THEIR NEW

LAND. THEY HAD LEARNED FROM THEIR FATHERS AND

GRANDFATHERS THAT THE BEST WAY TO PROTECT THEIR

CROPS WAS TO BUILD AND PUT OUT "BIRD BOXES" TO

ATTRACT INSECT-EATING BIRDS TO THEIR FIELDS AND

GARDENS. THE FARMERS USED WHATEVER MATERIALS

WERE CLOSE AT HAND—OLD BARN WOOD, CIGAR

BOXES, AND BARREL STAVES WERE FAVORITES.

DURING THE LONG WINTER MONTHS, WHEN THERE

WERE FEWER FARM CHORES, BUILDING BIRDHOUSES

BECAME A USEFUL PASTIME. A FARMER, TO RELIEVE

BOREDOM, MIGHT REPLICATE THE TOWN CHURCH, HIS

COW BARN, OR A NEIGHBOR'S FARMHOUSE INSTEAD OF

BUILDING A SIMPLE, UTILITARIAN BIRD BOX.

ORNAMENTAL BIRDHOUSES

IN THE VICTORIAN AGE, BIRDS—BECAUSE OF THEIR

PLUMAGE AND SONG—INSPIRED YET ANOTHER DECO-

RATIVE ELEMENT IN ALREADY FANCIFUL GARDENS.

DURING THIS ERA, WEALTHY LADIES AND GENTLEMEN

RETURNED FROM TRAVEL ABROAD WITH HUNDREDS OF

ENGLISH SPARROWS, AND IN THE MID-1800S BIRD-

HOUSES BECAME A FAVORITE FORM OF FOLLY. AS ELE-

GANT MANSIONS AROSE ALONG LOWER FIFTH AVENUE,

SO TOO DID ELEGANT BIRD MANSIONS. LOOKING LIKE

ELABORATE TIERED WEDDING CAKES, BIRDHOUSES

BUILT FOR A PARK OR PRIVATE GARDEN COULD HAVE A

DOZEN STORIES, PLUS STEEPLES, BALUSTRADES, AND

FINIALS TOPPING IT ALL.

A FEELING OF GOING BACK TO THAT EARLIER AND

MORE LEISURELY TIME CAN BE ENJOYED BY WALKING

AROUND GRAMERCY PARK IN NEW YORK CITY, WHERE

AMONG THE TREES AND FLOWERS BEHIND WROUGHT

IRON GATES DESCENDANTS OF THOSE GRAND OLD

BIRDHOUSES STILL PERCH HIGH ON CORBELED POSTS.

MULTI-FAMILY MARTIN HOUSES

IN CONTRAST TO THE DECORATIVE VICTORIAN

DOVECOTES AND SPARROW HOUSES OF THE CITIES AND

TOWNS, HOUSES BUILT BY FARMERS FOR MARTINS WERE

LIKE LARGE, HOMEY, MULTI-FAMILY ROOMING HOUSES.

A VERY SOCIAL BIRD, THE PURPLE MARTIN NOT

ONLY PREFERS TO LIVE IN A LARGE COLONY AMONG ITS

OWN SPECIES, BUT HAS A GENUINE AFFINITY FOR

PEOPLE AND FARM ANIMALS. ITS ORIGINAL NESTING

PREFERENCE WAS THE HOLLOWS OF DEAD TREES, BUT

URBANIZATION OF AMERICA AND MODERN LAND-
CLEARING PRACTICES ELIMINATED MOST OF THESE
NATURAL NESTING SITES. FORTUNATELY, FARMERS
HAVE ALWAYS APPRECIATED THE BENEFITS OF HAVING
MARTIN COLONIES ON THEIR FARMS AND HAVE BEEN

BUILDING HOUSES FOR THEM FOR DECADES.

LIKE PEOPLE, MARTINS SHOP CAREFULLY FOR A
HOUSE. IN THE EARLY SPRING, AFTER A WINTER SPENT
IN SOUTH AMERICA, THE MARTIN SCOUT, ALWAYS THE
MALE, CHECKS OUT "SUMMER RENTALS" FOR HIS MATE
AND THEIR LARGE EXTENDED FAMILY. THE SCOUT

LOOKS FOR A HOUSE THAT IS BIG AND WHITE, AND FURNISHED WITH MANY SEPARATE APARTMENTS, ONE FOR EACH FAMILY. THE HOUSE HAS TO BE BROOM CLEAN OR ON TO THE NEXT RENTAL HE WILL GO. HE LOOKS FOR A HOUSE THAT IS SAFE FROM PREDATORS, SET HIGH ON A POLE IN AN OPEN FIELD OR YARD, WITH NO NEARBY TREE BRANCHES FOR SQUIRRELS OR CATS TO LEAP FROM, AND PLENTY OF SPACE TO GRACEFULLY SWOOP IN AND OUT OF THE FRONT DOOR WITH FOOD FOR THE YOUNG.

WATER, OFTEN A BREEDING GROUND FOR MOS-QUITOES, IS MOST INVITING TO THE PURPLE MARTIN, WHO HAS AN ENORMOUS APPETITE AND FEEDS EX-CLUSIVELY ON FLYING INSECTS. IT IS NOT ONLY THE MARTIN'S DINING PREFERENCES AND CAPACITY THAT ENDEAR HIM TO FARMERS AND GARDENERS BUT HIS ABILITY TO DRIVE AWAY HAWKS AND CROWS FROM BARNYARDS AND HOMESTEADS.

Legend has it that the

more martins flitting

around an estate, the

greater the well-being

of its inhabitants.

BIRDHOUSES
IN GARDENS,
YARDS, AND
FIELDS

THE FORSYTHIA IS IN TENTATIVE BLOOM; THE DAYS
ARE GROWING LONGER. IT'S EARLY MARCH AND
THE ENTHUSIASTIC GARDENER IS MAKING READY
FOR SPRING. AFTER A WINTER SPENT
CONTEMPLATING THE TEMPTATIONS AND PROMISES
OF GARDEN CATALOGUES, THE HOUSE-
BOUND GARDENER IS ANXIOUS
TO GET OUT ON THE FIRST WARMISH
SPRING DAY AND DO SOMETHING!

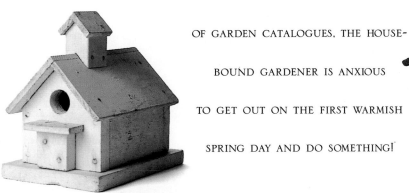

IN MOST PARTS OF THE COUNTRY, IT'S STILL TOO EARLY

TO PLANT, BUT IT IS THE PERFECT TIME TO READY THE

BIRDHOUSES FOR THE ARRIVAL OF THEIR NEW RESI-

DENTS. IT'S TIME TO CLEAN OUT THE OLD AND FIND

JUST THE RIGHT SPOT FOR A NEW BIRDHOUSE OR TWO

OR THREE. HOW WE LOOK FORWARD TO SPRING AND

THE RETURN OF BIRDS TO OUR GARDEN!

WE'RE LUCKY TO HAVE A BIG, OLD MULBERRY TREE

IN OUR BACKYARD; IT ATTRACTS HUNDREDS OF BIRDS

WHEN ITS BERRIES ARE RIPE. WE GIVE TIME AND

THOUGHT TO PROTECTING THE BIRDS, INVITING THEM

TO STAY IN OUR GARDEN WITH PLACES TO NEST AND

FEED AND BIRDBATHS TO SPLASH IN. WE DON'T USE

POISONS TO CONTROL INSECTS, INSTEAD LETTING THE

BIRDS EAT THEIR FILL. OF COURSE THEY DON'T GET

EVERY ONE, AND ON A WARM SUMMER EVENING THE

URGE TO USE A BUG BOMB CAN BE OVERWHELMING—

BUT THEN WE REMEMBER THE BABIES IN THE BIRD-

HOUSES. SINCE BIRDS EAT NEARLY THEIR WEIGHT IN

FOOD EVERY DAY, IT IS OUR GOAL TO ATTRACT ENOUGH

BIRDS TO OUR YARD TO FINISH OFF THE JOB.

OUR INTEREST IN BIRDHOUSES IS BOTH A DESIRE TO

HAVE BIRDS SINGING ABOUT THE GARDEN AND OUR

ENCHANTMENT AT SEEING A FUNNY LITTLE SHANTY ON

TOP OF AN ARBOR OR A WEATHERED COTTAGE TUCKED

INTO A THICKET OF ROSES. THESE MINIATURE HOUSES

ADD AN ARCHITECTURAL AND PLAYFUL DIMENSION TO

THE SMALLEST AND GRANDEST OF YARDS, GARDENS,

AND FIELDS.

Bird lovers from

Northern California to

eastern Long Island

create games of hide

and seek, surprising us

with whimsical yet

functional houses hidden

among the trees.

Well-weathered

birdhouses spend the

summer among black-

eyed Susans in

designer Lyn Peterson's

Westchester garden.

Not for function, but for

fun. A vintage birdhouse

sits on the table of a

child-sized Adirondack

settee in front of a

flowering border.

In a rural Maryland garden,

birdhouses and feeders, fences and

arbors are as much a part of the

colonial cottage design as are

flowers and plants.

From Oregon to

Massachusetts.

Washington state to

Maryland, birdhouse

fanciers show off their

favorites atop tall posts

and twiggy arbors.

A white steepled church,

a country farmhouse, a

tiny cottage, or a

hexagonal barn—all

architecture in miniature,

bringing humor and

birds to the garden.

Mabel Dodge Luhans

built her Taos estate in

the late 1920s with huge

wood dovecotes

dominating the front

garden walk.

A small chapel next to

El Sancturio de Chimayo

in New Mexico inspired

the adobe bird chapels

on the garden wall.

Berry bushes, thickets,

fruit trees, and

birdhousing are all an

integral part of the lush

eastern Long Island

gardens planted by a

master gardener to

nurture the birds.

BIRDHOUSES
ON HOUSES AND
IN HOUSES

THERE IS A DETOUR BIRDHOUSING

TAKES ON ITS WAY INTO THE

HOUSE FROM THE GARDEN. BIRDHOUSES

CAN BE SPOTTED IN A CUPOLA ON TOP OF

A HOUSE, NAILED TO THE SIDE OF A HOUSE—

EVEN DRILLED INTO PORCH COLUMNS.

ALL ARE INVITING TO A

VARIETY OF NESTING

BIRDS.

MANY PEOPLE BRING A BIRDHOUSE OR TWO—OR A

DOZEN—INSIDE AND LET FANTASY, NOT FUNCTION, BE

THEIR GUIDE. BIRDHOUSES OUTSIDE BRING BIRDS AND

ROMANCE TO A YARD OR GARDEN. INSIDE, BIRDHOUSES

BECOME FOLK ART WITH THE INTEGRITY TO BECOME

TOMORROW'S ANTIQUES.

SO MANY HOMES TODAY LACK ECCENTRICITY,

WHIMSY, OR ORNAMENTATION THAT A COLLECTION

BECOMES AN IMPORTANT STATEMENT OF ONE'S

UNIQUENESS. BIRDHOUSES—WITH THEIR HAND-

CRAFTED FLAWS AND QUIRKY DETAILS—APPEAL TO

THOSE OF US WHO WISH WE LIVED IN A CASTLE BUT, IN

FACT, LIVE IN A NEAT SHEETROCK HOUSE OR APART-

MENT OF THE TWENTIETH CENTURY.

WHAT IS SO APPEALING ABOUT THESE FOLK ART

RELICS? IS IT THEIR HUMOROUS DETAILS, THEIR

CLUMSY CHARM? IT MAY BE THAT FOR MOST OF US

WHO LOVE HOUSES, AND CAN CHOOSE ONLY ONE (OR

MAYBE TWO) TO LIVE IN, THE FUN OF ACQUIRING

HOUSE AFTER HOUSE — COTTAGE, LOG CABIN, GREEK

REVIVAL FARMHOUSE — WITHOUT HAVING TO GET A

MORTGAGE IS A DREAM COME TRUE.

Though the dovecote on this 1700s

early saltbox is a recent addition,

there may well have been an identical

one when the house was built.

Bird boxes on the side of Mary

Emmerling's cottage are a whimsical

play on tradition.

Not really inside but

not quite outside,

birdhouses rest on

tables on a screened-in

porch. Some are part

of the setting for an

afternoon snack.

Designer Lyn Peterson calls her birdhouse collection "life in miniature." Her

birdhousing pops up everywhere from the living room to her son's bookshelves.

A whimsical collection parades across a beam, and some rather serious

books are enlivened by some not-so-serious birdhouses.

A windowsill is home

to a town full of vintage

houses, picket fences

and all.

An antique house filling

a sunny window was

recycled from an old

nail barrel.

A simple weathered

house sits on a well-

polished wood table.

Several vintage

birdhouses peek out

here and there from an

old Welsh cupboard.

Shelves and sills hold

lots of things, from

dried hydrangeas and

Ball jars to the tiniest

possible birdhouse.

New folk art birdhouses

are favorites among

collectors.

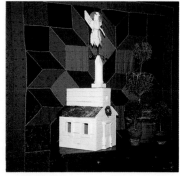

COLLECTING
BIRDHOUSES

THE PAINT IS PEELING,

A PORCH RAIL IS MISSING, THE DOOR

FRAME IS BADLY WORN, THERE IS NO

FURNACE. THIS HOUSE WOULD NEVER

PASS AN ENGINEER'S INSPECTION,

BUT FOR A BIRDHOUSE

COLLECTOR, IT'S A GEM.

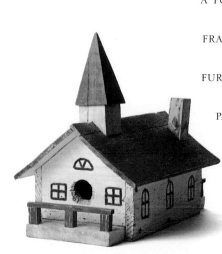

FOLK ART AND ANTIQUE BIRDHOUSES

MOST ANTIQUE BIRDHOUSES THAT EXIST TODAY ARE

LESS THAN SEVENTY-FIVE YEARS OLD. EARLIER EXAM-

PLES ARE RARE, SINCE THE STRUCTURES SAW HARD USE,

SPENDING YEAR AFTER YEAR IN SUN AND WIND AND

RAIN. RELATIVELY FEW BIRDHOUSES HAVE ENDURED

THE RAVAGES OF WEATHER AND TIME TO SURVIVE TO

THE PRESENT DAY.

WHAT APPEARS TO BE AN ORNATE VICTORIAN CAS-

TLE FROM THE 1890S COULD EASILY BE A REPRODUC-

TION BUILT AT A MUCH LATER DATE. HAVING

WEATHERED IN A GARDEN FOR ONLY A DECADE OR SO,

IT COULD HAVE ACQUIRED THE PATINA OF ANTIQUITY,

PLAYING TRICKS ON OUR SENSE OF TIME AND PLACE.

A COLLECTION DOESN'T HAVE TO BE OLD OR AN-

TIQUE TO BE GOOD FOLK ART. WHETHER OLD, MIDDLE-

AGED, OR VERY YOUNG, BIRDHOUSES FOUND AT CRAFT

SHOWS, COUNTRY ANTIQUE SHOPS, GALLERIES OF

PRIMITIVE ART, FLEA MARKETS, OR ONE OF THE MANY

OUTDOOR SUMMER ANTIQUE SHOWS CAN BE AFFORD-

ABLE, AND THE HUNT IS ALWAYS GREAT FUN.

These great old relics

of martin rooming

houses have lots of

detail and pleasantly

peeling paint.

BIRDHOUSES
FOR CHRISTMAS

IT'S CHRISTMASTIME AND THE LUCKIEST BIRDS HAVE

GONE SOUTH FOR THE WINTER, LEAVING THEIR

HOUSES EMPTY UNTIL SPRING. HOUSES THAT WERE

ONCE HIDDEN AMONG THE FOLIAGE OF SUMMER NOW

STAND OUT BRIGHTLY AGAINST THE BARE WINTER

LANDSCAPE, CHEERING AN OTHERWISE DRAB GARDEN.

WHEN IT SNOWS, A WELCOME TREAT IN NEW ENGLAND

THESE PAST FEW WINTERS, THE BIRDHOUSES IN OUR

YARD ARE A MAGICAL SIGHT.

ALL THROUGH THE WINTER THERE ARE BIRDS IN

OUR YARD. THOUGH THEY DON'T NEST IN HOUSES, THIS

HEARTY, BRIGHTLY COLORED GROUP OF BIRDS STAYS UP NORTH, EATING BERRIES AND GRAINS LEFT FROM SUMMER. BLUE JAYS, CARDINALS, AND WOODPECKERS ARE HAPPY TO FEED FROM SEED STARS THAT DECORATE OUR SMALL SPRUCE TREE FOR THE HOLIDAYS, THE GRAIN AND NUT WREATH ON THE BARN DOOR, AND THE ASSORTED FEEDERS OUTSIDE THE KITCHEN WINDOW.

INSIDE, THOSE SPECIAL BIRDHOUSES WE COLLECT ARE DECORATED WITH GRAPEVINE NAPKIN RINGS PRESSED INTO SERVICE AS WREATHS FOR THEIR FRONT OPENINGS. ON CHRISTMAS DAY IN THE CITY WE PUT RUSTIC BIRDHOUSES ON OUR BUFFET TABLE. TRIMMED WITH WREATHS AND GOLD RIBBONS, AND SET ON A BED OF FRESH GREEN LEAVES, THEY CREATE AN ENCHANTING CENTERPIECE. MINIATURE BIRDHOUSES AND BIRD NESTS ARE AN UNEXPECTED SURPRISE AMONG THE LIGHTS ON OUR CHRISTMAS TREES, CONTRASTING NATURAL, EARTHY ELEMENTS WITH THE SPARKLE OF THE HOLIDAY SEASON.

BIRDHOUSE
BUILDERS
OF TODAY

Building birdhouses is a continuing

tradition. As in earlier times, today's builders

look to their own backyards for inspiration.

They use materials at hand, like weathered

shutters, old roof shingles, or bits and pieces

of fallen-down shakes. The houses they build

are in the local vernacular.

And so this architecture

for the birds reflects the

architecture of the nation.

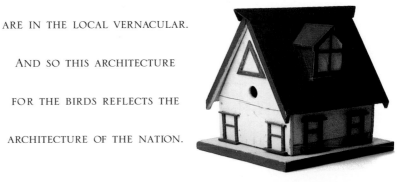

LEON GOBILLOT

DRIVING NORTH THROUGH RURAL CONNECTICUT WE

SPOTTED A MODEST RANCH HOUSE SURROUNDED BY

LAWN, A SPLIT-RAIL FENCE, AND HIGH MARSH GRASSES.

WHAT CAUGHT OUR FANCY WERE DOZENS OF SMALL,

COLORFUL BIRDHOUSES ON EVERY FENCE POST, IN

EVERY TREE, ON EVERY STUMP. THEN WE SAW THE

SMALL, HANDPAINTED SIGN IN FRONT THAT SAID

"BIRDHOUSES FOR SALE."

THE SIGN WAS AN OPEN INVITATION. LEON, A RE-

TIRED FARMER WHO WAS BROUGHT UP IN THE BIG

FARMHOUSE ACROSS THE ROAD, WAS HAPPY TO VISIT

WITH US AND TO TALK ABOUT HIS BIRDHOUSES. HIS

BIGGEST AND OLDEST HOUSE WAS GIVEN TO HIM BY ITS

BUILDER, WHO IS NOW 102 YEARS OLD.

LEON BUILDS BIRDHOUSES AS A HOBBY, THOUGH

HE'S HAPPY TO SELL THE OCCASIONAL HOUSE. BECAUSE

HIS PROPERTY IS SURROUNDED BY WETLANDS AND HIS

HOUSES ARE SO INVITING, THEY ATTRACT A GREAT

RANGE OF BIRDS. WE MOST ENVY HIS VISITING EASTERN

BLUEBIRDS. ONCE AS COMMON AS ROBINS, THE BLUE-

BIRDS OF HAPPINESS ARE A RARE SIGHT TODAY.

PETERO RUGGIERA

WE FOUND THE NEW ENGLAND FARMHOUSE WE HAD

ALWAYS WANTED: WHITE CLAPBOARD, TWO STORIES

HIGH, WITH A NICE PITCH TO THE ROOF. THERE WERE A

DOZEN MARTIN HOUSES IN THE FIELD SURROUNDING

PETE AND IRENE RUGGIERA'S LITTLE FARMHOUSE.

PETE, A RETIRED ARMY OFFICER, BUILDS BIRD-

HOUSES OUT OF WOOD SCRAPS IN HIS BACKYARD AND

GROWS GIANT SUNFLOWERS IN THE FRONT YARD. HE

STARTED US BIRDHOUSING AND GAVE US OUR EDUCA-

TION ABOUT THE PURPLE MARTIN.

VIDAL SISNEROS

THEY'RE NOT FOR SALE, BUT ANY COLLECTOR WOULD

WISH THEY WERE. PERCHED ON POSTS IN VIDAL SIS-

NEROS'S YARD IN TAOS, NEW MEXICO, ARE TWO

SOUTHWESTERN, FRONTIER-STYLE BIRDHOUSES. ONE

IS STRUNG WITH CHRISTMAS LIGHTS, YEAR-ROUND.

A NATIVE OF NEW MEXICO, VIDAL RETIRED FROM

THE DEPARTMENT OF HIGHWAYS AND HAS BEEN BUSY

FILLING HIS HOUSE AND YARD WITH HIS HANDIWORK

EVER SINCE. VIDAL DOESN'T THINK OF HIMSELF AS A

FOLK ARTIST, BUT BY OUR DEFINITION HE IS.

DEAN JOHNSON

THERE IS ONE MAIN STREET IN KEEDYSVILLE, MARY-

LAND, AND IF YOU DRIVE TOO FAST, YOU'LL MISS IT. SO

WE DROVE SLOWLY DOWN THIS PRETTY, HISTORIC

STREET IN THE HEART OF A CIVIL WAR BATTLEFIELD TO

ITS VERY END, NOT EVEN A MILE, TO DEAN JOHNSON

AND JIMMY CRAMER'S HOUSE.

ON THAT WARM FALL DAY EVERYTHING ABOUT

THEIR HOUSE AND GARDENS SPOKE OF HISTORY AND

TRADITION. THEIR HOUSE IS FILLED WITH FOLK ART,

OLD AND NEW. THEIR GARDENS HAVE NEAT BOXWOOD

HEDGES, WEATHERED PICKET FENCES, GAZEBOS, AND

DOZENS OF BIRDHOUSES AND FEEDERS.

THERE'S A SMALL BARN AT THE EDGE OF THE GAR-

DEN WHERE DEAN PAINSTAKINGLY CONSTRUCTS LOG

CABINS AND CLAPBOARD FARMHOUSES FOR BIRDS. IN

THE BEST TRADITION OF THE SOUTH NO DETAIL IS LEFT

OUT. THERE ARE CHIMNEYS AND FRONT PORCHES. THE

WINDOWS AND DOORS ARE CAREFULLY TRIMMED.

SOME HOUSES HAVE WEATHERVANES. THEY ARE SO

WELL BUILT AND SO BEAUTIFUL WE WISHED DEAN

WOULD BUILD ONE FOR US TO LIVE IN.

PEGGY FRUEHLING

PEGGY FRUEHLING INTRODUCED HERSELF AND HER BIRDHOUSES TO US THROUGH THE MAIL. AFTER OUR INTRODUCTION, WHENEVER A CARTON FROM PEGGY ARRIVED AT THE STORE, EVERYONE WAS ANXIOUS TO SEE WHAT HER QUIRKY LITTLE COTTAGES WOULD BE LIKE THIS TIME. NO TWO WERE EVER ALIKE, AND THERE WAS ALWAYS ONE WE JUST HAD TO KEEP.

AFTER TWO YEARS OF CORRESPONDENCE, WE WENT TO THE PACIFIC NORTHWEST TO MEET PEGGY. DRIVING UP THE COAST OF OREGON TOWARD PEGGY'S HOUSE, WE COULD IMMEDIATELY SEE THE INSPIRATION FOR HER BIRDHOUSES IN THE TURN-OF-THE-CENTURY VICTORIAN COTTAGES THAT DOTTED THE COAST ROAD.

PEGGY AND HER PARTNER BILL GOODRICH CONSTRUCT ROWS OF LITTLE SHANTIES. USING SCRAP FROM AN ABANDONED HOUSE NEARBY, THEY SALVAGE PIECES OF MOLDING, SHINGLES, SCREENING, AND ODD ADORNMENTS THAT TURN HER HOUSES INTO THE MOST DISARMING AND COLLECTIBLE COTTAGES.

FRED VAN ANDA

THE FOLK ARTIST IS AN INVENTIVE MAN. HE HATES

WASTE; HE IS RELUCTANT TO DISCARD ANYTHING.

THAT'S FRED VAN ANDA, ALL RIGHT.

WHEN WE VISITED FRED AND DEBBY VAN ANDA AT

THEIR HOMESTEAD IN NORTHERN CALIFORNIA'S GOLD

MINING COUNTRY, WE WERE OVERWHELMED BY HIS

CACHE OF RAW MATERIALS. ALL WERE SALVAGE,

STACKED NEATLY BY CATEGORY IN A DISCARDED BOX

CAR. THERE WERE PILES OF CORRUGATED ROOFING,

FOR WHICH FRED HAS RIGGED A "STEAM ROLLER" TO

FLATTEN OUT THE RIPPLES. AGAINST ANOTHER WALL

WERE BARN BOARDS IN EVERY WEATHER-FADED HUE

IMAGINABLE. THERE WERE BUCKETS OF OLD SQUARE

NAILS, STACKS OF SHUTTERS, AND DISCARDED TO-

BACCO POSTS.

THE BIRDHOUSES FRED VAN ANDA BUILDS ARE

MADE FROM AND INSPIRED BY THE RUGGED UN-

PAINTED BARNS OF HIS NATIVE CALIFORNIA, AND ARE

A TESTAMENT TO HIS INGENUITY.

LAURA FOREMAN

WE THOUGHT BIRDHOUSE BUILDING WAS STRICTLY A

COUNTRY CRAFT UNTIL WE SAW THE BIRDHOUSES OF

NEW YORK CITY ARTIST LAURA FOREMAN. LAURA

THINKS OF HER HOUSES — WHICH HAVE BEEN BUILT

FOR FIVE MANHATTAN

VEST-POCKET PARKS — AS

METAPHORS FOR URBAN

LIFE. THEY PROBABLY

BRING A SMILE TO MANY

A NEW YORKER WHO DREAMS OF BEING FREE AS A BIRD.

A TURN-OF-THE-CENTURY TENEMENT ON WEST 48TH

STREET WAS LAURA'S INSPIRATION FOR THE TENEMENT

BIRDHOUSE SHE BUILT AND INSTALLED IN CLINTON

GARDEN, A SMALL NEIGHBORHOOD PARK DIRECTLY

ACROSS THE STREET.

FEED AND SEED

"YOU EAT LIKE A BIRD" ISN'T A COMPLIMENT;

BIRDS EAT NEARLY THEIR WEIGHT

IN FOOD EVERY DAY. THAT'S A LOT

OF WORK, FLYING AROUND CATCHING INSECTS,

JUMPING FROM BRANCH TO BRANCH EATING BERRIES,

DIGGING IN THE GROUND FOR WORMS. IT'S

EASY TO UNDERSTAND WHY A BIRD

WOULD BE ATTRACTED TO GARDENS WHERE

A STEADY SUPPLEMENTAL FOOD SUPPLY

COULD BE COUNTED ON YEAR-ROUND.

IN THE EARLY SPRING, MOST PREFERRED NATURAL
FOODS HAVE BEEN CONSUMED OVER THE WINTER BY
NONMIGRATORY BIRDS. FULL FEEDERS WILL TEMPT
BIRDS TO STICK AROUND AND NEST IN A WELCOMING
NEIGHBORHOOD.

SUMMER, THE SEASON WITH THE MOST ABUNDANCE
OF NATURAL FOOD, IS ALSO THE TIME OF GREATEST
NEED. PARENTS WORK FROM DAWN TO DUSK CATCHING
INSECTS TO FEED THEIR YOUNG, WHOSE MOUTHS ARE
ALWAYS OPEN. FEEDERS PROVIDE THE PARENTS WITH A
READY SUPPLY OF FAST, NUTRITIOUS FOOD.

FALL FEEDING CAN HELP YOUNG MIGRATORY AND

NONMIGRATORY BIRDS SURVIVE THE FIRST HARD YEAR

OF LIFE. SUPPLEMENTAL FEEDING COULD MAKE THE

DIFFERENCE FOR A BIRD THAT MIGHT OTHERWISE NOT

BUILD UP ENOUGH FAT FOR THE MIGRATION.

WINTER IS THE MOST DIFFICULT SEASON FOR BIRDS.

IN MANY NORTHERN AREAS THE GROUND IS FROZEN,

THE SUPPLY OF BERRIES AND SEEDS DWINDLES, AND

THERE ARE NO INSECTS AT ALL. IN WINTER THE RESI-

DENT BIRDS — CARDINALS, BLUE JAYS, AND

SPARROWS — ARE CONSTANT DINERS AT OUR FEEDERS.

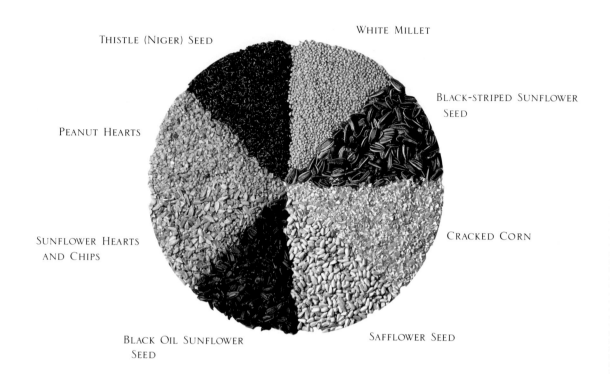

THISTLE (NIGER) SEED

WHITE MILLET

BLACK-STRIPED SUNFLOWER SEED

PEANUT HEARTS

SUNFLOWER HEARTS AND CHIPS

CRACKED CORN

BLACK OIL SUNFLOWER SEED

SAFFLOWER SEED

"God gave a loaf to

every bird, but just

a crumb to me."

— Emily Dickinson

Crunchy Peanut Butter "Cake"

3 CUPS RENDERED SUET OR BACON FAT
2 CUPS COARSELY CHOPPED PEANUTS
1 CUP PEANUT BUTTER (ANY KIND)
1 CUP SUNFLOWER HEARTS

WARM THE SUET OR BACON FAT IN A SAUCEPAN. MIX ALL INGREDIENTS THOROUGHLY. WITH YOUR HANDS. MOLD INTO "CUPCAKES." PLACE CAKES IN THE CURVE OF A GRAPE-VINE WREATH HUNG ON A TREE. OR PUT THEM INSIDE A BIRD FEEDER BAG OR SUET HOLDER.

Fresh Fruit Salad

GRAPEFRUIT BY ITSELF ISN'T VERY POPULAR WITH BIRDS. BUT EMPTIED GRAPEFRUIT HALVES ARE READY-MADE BOWLS FOR FRUIT SALADS. WHICH MANY BIRDS LOVE. YOU CAN LEAVE THE MIXTURE OUT AS LONG AS IT'S EDIBLE IN BIRD TERMS — VERY SOFT OR BROWN FRUIT DOESN'T BOTHER THEM. BUT KEEP AN EYE OUT AND THROW IT AWAY BEFORE MOLD OR ROT SETS IN.

CHOP UP ANY COMBINATION OF ORANGES. GRAPES. AP-PLES, BERRIES, MELONS, OR BANANAS. MIX THE FRESH FRUIT WITH ANY JUICES AND WHATEVER CHOPPED DRIED FRUITS — PRUNES. FIGS. DATES. CURRANTS. RAISINS — YOU HAVE ON HAND. PILE THE SALAD INTO HOLLOWED-OUT HALVES OF GRAPEFRUIT OR MELON AND PUT OUT ON A FEEDING TABLE OR ON THE SHELF OF A FEEDER.

BUYER'S GUIDE
HOUSES AND ACCESSORIES

California

CARMEL BAY COMPANY

P.O. Box 5606
Ocean Avenue and Lincoln Street
Carmel, CA 93921
(408) 624-3868
Home furnishings, rustic birdhouses, accessories for the home
and garden.

THE GARDENER

1836 Fourth Street
Berkeley, CA 94710
(510) 548-4545
Furniture for the gardener's home
and garden, birdhouses and supplies,
equipment for al fresco dining.

SWEET WILLIAM

1661 Sunflower Avenue
South Coast Plaza Village
Santa Ana, CA 92704
(714) 966-2722
Vintage accessories for cottage
and garden, including birdhouses.

WILD GOOSE CHASE

1631 Sunflower Avenue
South Coast Plaza Village
Santa Ana, CA 92704
(714) 966-2722
Antique model houses, early painted
furniture, quilts, birdhouses.

Connecticut

BIRDNEST OF RIDGEFIELD

2 Big Shop Lane
Ridgefield, CT 06877
(203) 431-9889
General store for birders—
birdhouses, binoculars, gifts, garden accessories.

Idaho

MICHEL'S ANTIQUES

Trail Creek Village
Ketchum, ID 83340
(208) 726-8382
Antique and new birdhouses, French
country antiques.

Illinois

ART EFFECT

651 West Armitage
Chicago, IL 60614
(312) 664-0997
Birdhouses, home accessories.

Maryland

FEATHERS AND LACE

8133 MAIN STREET
ELLICOTT CITY, MD 21043
(410) 313-8827
BIRDHOUSES, HOME AND GARDEN
ACCESSORIES.

Massachusetts

LA RUCHE

168 NEWBURY STREET
BOSTON, MA 02116
(617) 536-6366
BIRDHOUSES, GARDEN ORNAMENTS, DEC-
ORATIVE ACCESSORIES.

THE SPLENDID PEASANT

ROUTE 23
SOUTH EGREMONT, MA 01258
(413) 528-5755
MUSEUM-QUALITY AMERICAN FOLK ART,
EARLY PAINTED FURNITURE, ANTIQUE
BIRDHOUSES.

T.P. SADDLE BLANKET & TRADING CO.

304 MAIN STREET
GREAT BARRINGTON, MA 01230
(413) 528-6500
SOUTHWESTERN GENERAL STORE, RUSTIC
BIRDHOUSES, TABLEWARE, BEDDING, AND
WESTERN GEAR.

Missouri

PASTIME ANTIQUES

BOX 102
HIGHWAY 190
JAMESPORT, MO 64648
(816) 684-6222

EARLY PRIMITIVE ANTIQUES, PAINTED
PIECES, QUILTS, DECORATIVE ITEMS,
BIRDHOUSES.

New York

AMERICAN PRIMITIVE GALLERY

596 BROADWAY #205
NEW YORK, NY 10012
(212) 966-1530
AMERICAN FOLK ART (NINETEENTH AND
TWENTIETH CENTURY) — BIRDHOUSES,
DECOYS, COUNTRY FURNITURE, SCULP-
TURE, UTILITARIAN OBJECTS.

DEVONSHIRE

P.O. BOX 1860
MAIN STREET
BRIDGEHAMPTON, NY 11932
(516) 537- 2661
DECORATIVE ACCESSORIES FOR HOME
AND GARDEN, BIRDHOUSES.

GEORGICA CREEK ANTIQUES

P.O. BOX 877
MONTAUK HIGHWAY
WAINSCOTT, NY 11975
(516) 537-0333
ANTIQUE LARGE-SCALE BIRDHOUSES, EN-
GLISH AND AMERICAN FURNITURE,
QUILTS, GARDEN FURNITURE.

LEXINGTON GARDENS

1008 LEXINGTON AVENUE
NEW YORK, NY 10021
(212) 861-4390
BIRDHOUSES, GARDEN ORNAMENTS AND
FURNITURE, DRIED ARRANGEMENTS.

CHRIS MEAD'S
ENGLISH COUNTRY ANTIQUES

SNAKE HOLLOW ROAD
BRIDGEHAMPTON, NY 11932
(516) 537-0606
RUSTIC BIRDHOUSES, HERB GARDEN, EN-
GLISH FURNITURE, GARDEN ACCESSORIES.

MORGAN RANK GALLERY

4 NEWTOWN LANE
EAST HAMPTON, NY 11937
(516) 324-7615
AMERICAN PRIMITIVE ART AND ANTIQUES.

WOLFMAN • GOLD & GOOD COMPANY

116 GREENE STREET
NEW YORK, NY 10012
(212) 431-1888
BIRDHOUSES, SEED WREATHS, CHRISTMAS
DECORATIONS, CHINA, LINEN, GLASS-
WARE, ANTIQUES.

Oregon

MORELAND HOUSE N.W.

826 N.W. 23RD AVENUE
PORTLAND, OR 97210
(503) 222-0197
ANTIQUES, PRIMITIVES, FOLK ART,
BIRDHOUSES.

Pennsylvania

DILWORTHTOWN COUNTRY STORE

275 BRINTONS BRIDGE ROAD
WEST CHESTER, PA 19382
(215) 399-0560
EIGHTEENTH-CENTURY DECORATIVE
ACCESSORIES, FOLK ART, BIRDHOUSES,
DECOYS.

Virginia

DEVONSHIRE

6 NORTH MADISON STREET
P.O. BOX 760
MIDDLEBURG, VA 22117
(703) 687-5990
DECORATIVE ACCESSORIES FOR HOME
AND GARDEN, BIRDHOUSES.

NANCY THOMAS GALLERY

145 BALLARD STREET
YORKTOWN, VA 23690
(804) 898-3665
NEW AND ANTIQUE FOLK ART, BIRD-
HOUSES, ACCESSORIES. CATALOGUE
AVAILABLE.

CATALOGUES

AUDUBON WORKSHOP

1501 PADDOCK DRIVE
NORTHBROOK, IL 60062
(800) 325-9464
SEED, SUET, FEEDERS, HOUSES, BATHS,
BOOKS.

BACKYARD BIRDS & CO.

717 S. BROADVIEW ROAD
SPRINGFIELD, MO 65809
(417) 869-4788
SEED, FEED, FEEDERS, HOUSES.

BIRD'N HAND INC.

40 PEARL STREET
FRAMINGHAM, MA 01701
(508) 879-1552
SEED, FEED, FEEDERS, INFORMATIVE
NEWSLETTER.

Dakota Quality Bird Feed

Box 3084
Fargo, ND 58108
(800) 356-9220
Seed, feeders, feed, houses.

Droll Yankees Inc.

27 Mill Road
Foster, RI 02825
(401) 647-3324
Feeders, hooks, books.

Duncraft

Penacook, NH 03303
(603) 224-0200
Seed, feed, feeders, houses, books, telescoping poles. Manufacturers of National Audubon Society products.

Gardener's Eden

Mail Order Department
P.O. Box 7307
San Francisco, CA 94120
(800) 822-9600
Decorative accessories for home and garden, furniture, garden tools, wreaths, birdhouses.

Maine Manna

P.O. Box 248
Gorham, ME 04038
(207) 839-6013
Suet and seed bells, seed dispensers.

Meta Nature Products

c/o Tim Lundquist
56 Walkers Hill
Tivoli, NY 12583
(518) 828-0533
Information on ordering the estate wild bird feeder shown on page 88.

The Nature Company

750 Hearst Avenue
Berkeley, CA 94710
(800) 227-1114
Paraphernalia for naturalists, including birdhouses, birdfeeders, optical equipment, books.

Old Elm Feed & Supplies

Box 825
13400 Watertown Plank Road
Elm Grove, WI 53122
(800) 782-3300
Seed, feeders, feed, houses.

Smith & Hawken

25 Corte Madera
Mill Valley, CA 94941
(415) 383-2000
Garden tools, seeds and bulbs, furniture and accessories, birdhouses and feeders.

Wild Bird Supplies

4815 Oak Street
Crystal Lake, IL 60012
(815) 455-4020
Seed, feed, feeders, houses.

WOLFMAN•GOLD & GOOD COMPANY

116 GREENE STREET

NEW YORK, NY 10012

(212) 431-1888

BIRDHOUSES, FEEDERS, SEED ORNAMENTS,
HOME FURNISHINGS.

SUGGESTED READING

ATTRACTING PURPLE MARTINS, BY J. L.
WADE. THE NATURE SOCIETY, PURPLE
MARTIN JUNCTION, GRIGGSVILLE, IL
62340, 1987.

FROM THE PURPLE MARTIN CAPITAL OF
THE UNITED STATES, THIS BOOK TELLS
EVERYTHING YOU COULD POSSIBLY WANT
TO KNOW ABOUT THE PURPLE MARTIN.

THE BEST NEST, BY P. D. EASTMAN. NEW
YORK: RANDOM HOUSE, 1968.

A DR. SEUSS–LIKE CHILDREN'S BOOK
ABOUT MR. AND MRS. BIRD'S QUEST FOR
THE PERFECT HOUSE.

BIRD, AN EYEWITNESS BOOK, WRITTEN BY
DAVID BURNIE, PHOTOGRAPHED BY
PETER CHADWICK. NEW YORK: ALFRED A.
KNOPF, 1988.

A WONDERFULLY INFORMATIVE, BEAU-
TIFULLY PHOTOGRAPHED BOOK ABOUT
BIRD ANATOMY AND HABITS WITH INFOR-
MATION ABOUT A FEW BASIC BIRDHOUSES.

THE BIRD HOUSE BOOK, BY BRUCE
WOODS AND DAVID SCHOONMAKER. NEW
YORK: STERLING PUBLISHING, 1991.

A CREATIVE BOOK ABOUT HOW TO BUILD
YOUR OWN BIRDHOUSES AND FEEDERS.

DECORATING EDEN, EDITED BY ELIZ-
ABETH WILKINSON AND MARJORIE HEN-
DERSON, SAN FRANCISCO: CHRONICLE
BOOKS, 1992.

A COMPREHENSIVE SOURCEBOOK OF
CLASSIC GARDEN DESIGN AND
ARCHITECTURE.

FEED THE BIRDS, BY HELEN WITTY AND
DICK WITTY. NEW YORK: WORKMAN PUB-
LISHING, 1991.

AN AMUSING AND INFORMATION-FILLED
BOOK ON FEEDING BIRDS, INCLUDING
RECIPES FOR MAKING BIRD TREATS AND A
NET BAG TO HANG THEM IN.

GARDEN BIRDS—HOW TO ATTRACT
BIRDS TO YOUR GARDEN, BY DR. NOBLE
PROCTOR. EMMAUS, PENN.: RODALE
PRESS, 1986.

A DELIGHTFUL BOOK WITH LOTS OF IN-
FORMATION ABOUT ATTRACTING BIRDS
TO YOUR GARDEN AND FEEDING THEM.
IT ALSO HAS EXCELLENT INFORMATION
ABOUT WHICH BIRDS NEST IN HOUSES
AND THEIR REQUIREMENTS.